New Orleans

New Orleans

A Downtown America Book

Joan Kane Nichols

Dillon Press
New York

Collier Macmillan Canada
Toronto

Maxwell Macmillan International Publishing Group
New York   Oxford   Singapore   Sydney

Library of Congress Cataloging-in-Publication Data

Nichols, Joan Kane.

New Orleans / Joan Kane Nichols.

p. cm. — (A Downtown America book)

Includes index.

Summary: Explores New Orleans as a major port and cultural center, describing its history, neighborhoods, people, traditions, and celebrations.

ISBN 0-87518-403-0

1. New Orleans (La.)—Juvenile literature. [1. New Orleans (La.)] I. Title. II. Series.

F379.N54N53 1989

976.3'35—dc 19   88-35915
                                         CIP
                                         AC

Macmillan Publishing Company, 866 Third Avenue
New York, NY 10022

Printed in the United States of America
  2 3 4 5 6 7 8 9 10

For Dwayne

Photographic Acknowledgments

The photographs have been reproduced through the courtesy of Toby Armstrong, Dwayne Campbell, D. Donne Bryant Stock Photography Agency, Louisiana Office of Tourism, and Orleans Photography (Susan Leavines).

Contents

Fast Facts about New Orleans

New Orleans: The Crescent City; The City that Care Forgot; The Big Easy

Location: Southeastern Louisiana, on the banks of the Mississippi River about 107 miles (172 kilometers) above its mouth

Area: City, land area of 197 square miles (510 square kilometers); metropolitan area, 1,967 square miles (5,095 square kilometers), including the parishes of Orleans, Jefferson, St. Bernard, and St. Tammany. (In Louisiana, a parish is similar to a county.)

Population (1986 estimate*): City, 554,500; metropolitan area, 1,332,900

Major Population Groups: Blacks, Creoles (of French or Spanish ancestry), Germans, Irish, Italians, Cajuns, Vietnamese

Altitude: Sea level; highest—natural levee along the Mississippi River, 15 feet (4.5 meters); lowest—5 feet (1.5 meters) below sea level

Climate: Average annual temperature is 57°F (13°C) in January, 83°F (28°C) in July; average annual precipitation is more than 60 inches (150 centimeters)

Founding Date: 1718, incorporated as a city in 1805

City Flag: Adopted 1918; three golden fleurs-de-lis (irises) representing the city's French origins on a white background, with a red stripe above and a blue stripe below. The color white represents purity in government, red represents fraternity, and blue liberty.

*U.S. Bureau of the Census 1988 population estimates available in fall 1989; official 1990 census figures available in 1991-92.

City Seal: Adopted 1852; below the words *City of New Orleans*, an Indian man and woman stand on either side of a shield. On the shield, Neptune (representing the Mississippi River) greets the rising sun. A circle of 25 stars above the shield and 3 stars on either side represent the 31 states admitted into the Union by 1850. An alligator at the bottom of the seal recalls the Louisiana swamps.

Form of Government: The city shares its boundaries with Orleans Parish. Both are governed by a mayor and a city council.

Important Industries: Port and its trade, tourism, petroleum refining, ship and boat building, sugar production

Festivals and Parades

February: Mardi Gras

March: St. Patrick's Day Parade; St. Joseph's Day

April: Spring Fiesta; French Quarter Festival; New Orleans Jazz and Heritage Festival

June: New Orleans Food Festival

July: La Fête; Bastille Day

October: Festa d'Italia; Halloween Happenings

December: Creole Christmas; New Year's Eve Countdown

For further information about festivals and parades, see agencies listed on page 56.

United States

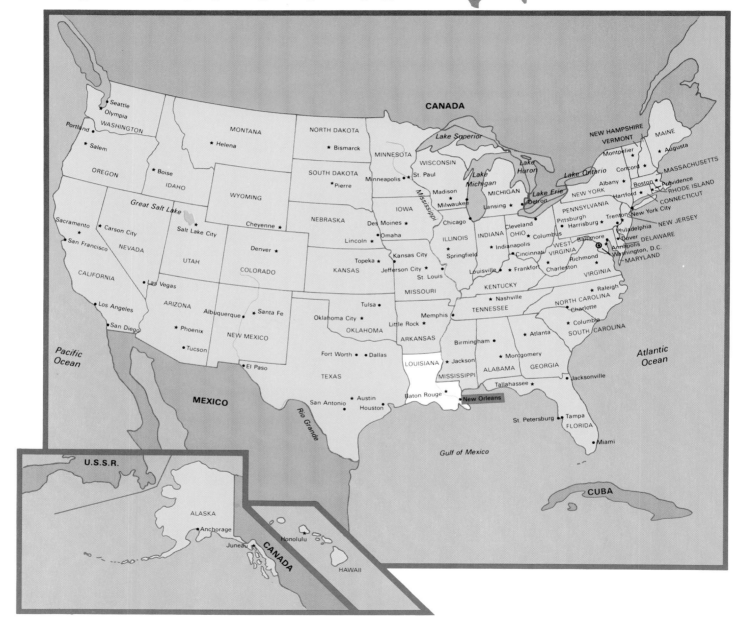

New Orleans

LOUISIANA
New Orleans

LAKE PONTCHARTRAIN

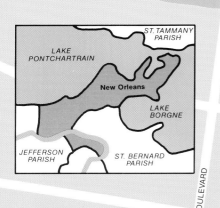

ST. TAMMANY PARISH
LAKE PONTCHARTRAIN
New Orleans
LAKE BORGNE
JEFFERSON PARISH
ST. BERNARD PARISH

N

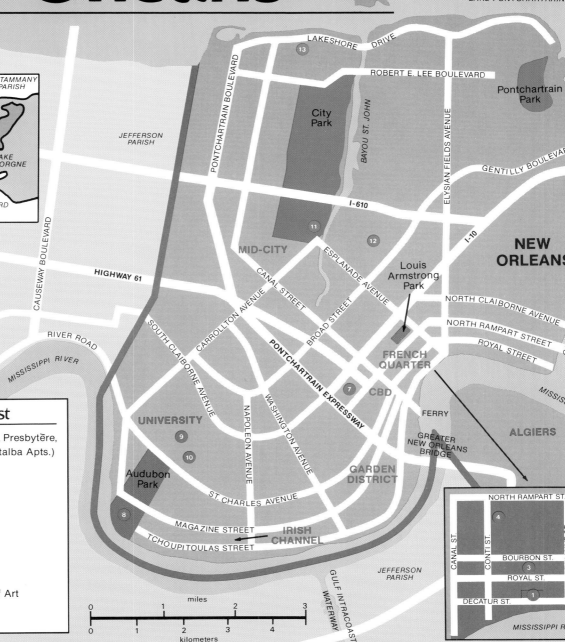

LAKESHORE DRIVE
ROBERT E. LEE BOULEVARD
Pontchartrain Park
INNER HARBOR NAVIGATION CANAL
PONTCHARTRAIN BOULEVARD
City Park
BAYOU ST. JOHN
ELYSIAN FIELDS AVENUE
GENTILLY BOULEVARD
JEFFERSON PARISH
I-610
I-10
NEW ORLEANS
GULF INTRACOASTAL WATERWAY
MID-CITY
ESPLANADE AVENUE
HIGHWAY 61
CANAL STREET
BROAD STREET
Louis Armstrong Park
NORTH CLAIBORNE AVENUE
NORTH RAMPART STREET
CARROLLTON AVENUE
ROYAL STREET
RIVER ROAD
CAUSEWAY BOULEVARD
SOUTH CLAIBORNE AVENUE
PONTCHARTRAIN EXPRESSWAY
FRENCH QUARTER
MISSISSIPPI RIVER
MISSISSIPPI RIVER
CBD
FERRY
ALGIERS
UNIVERSITY
NAPOLEON AVENUE
WASHINGTON AVENUE
GREATER NEW ORLEANS BRIDGE
Audubon Park
GARDEN DISTRICT
ST. CHARLES AVENUE
MAGAZINE STREET
IRISH CHANNEL
TCHOUPITOULAS STREET
JEFFERSON PARISH
GULF INTRACOASTAL WATERWAY

Points of Interest

1. Jackson Square (Cabildo, Presbytère, St. Louis Cathedral, Pontalba Apts.)
2. French Market
3. Preservation Hall
4. Musée Conti
5. Voodoo Museum
6. Old U.S. Mint Building
7. Louisiana Superdome
8. Audubon Zoo
9. Tulane University
10. Loyola University
11. New Orleans Museum of Art
12. Fairgrounds
13. Mardi Gras Fountain

miles
0   1   2   3
0   1   2   3   4
kilometers

NORTH RAMPART ST.
CANAL ST.
CONTI ST.
DUMAINE ST.
ESPLANADE AVE.
BOURBON ST.
ROYAL ST.
DECATUR ST.
MISSISSIPPI RIVER

1

Welcome to the Crescent City

Without the Mississippi River, New Orleans probably wouldn't exist. The city was born on the river and grew in size, wealth, and importance around it. Without the river, New Orleans wouldn't be the largest city in Louisiana. The river brought it a variety of people: Creoles, Cajuns, blacks, whites, Irish, Germans, Italians, and more.

The Mississippi River runs north to south down the center of the United States. Near the end of the river, on the southeastern tip of Louisiana, lies New Orleans. This important port is less than 50 miles (80 kilometers) west of the Gulf of Mexico. Lake Pontchartrain forms a natural border to the north of the city, the river to the south. As the Mississippi curves around New Orleans, it forms the outline of a new moon, or crescent. This outline gives the city one of

A view of New Orleans from the air shows how the Mississippi River curves around the city.

its nicknames—the "Crescent City."

Because New Orleans is in the Deep South and near the gulf, its climate is semi-tropical. The city has short, mild winters, but this pleasant weather is followed by long, hot, humid summers. Each summer day, dehumidifiers throughout the city fill up with water pulled from the moist air. Only the frequent thunderstorms offer relief from the sticky heat.

Citizens of New Orleans must also adapt to their city's swampy location. Much of the city lies below sea level—five feet (1.5 meters) below at the lowest point. Because water lies just beneath the ground's surface, the land is extremely marshy. If it weren't for the pumps and canals that drain billions of gallons of water from the

New Orleanians like to relax during the city's long, hot, humid summers.

The historic St. Louis Cemetery is famous for its aboveground mausoleums.

city almost every day, New Orleanians would spend much of their time sloshing through muddy streets in waist-high rubber boots.

Over the years, residents have drained large areas of swamp to create land to build on. But water remains just a few feet below ground, so houses and other buildings are constructed without basements. For the same reason, very few graves are dug in New Orleans soil. Instead, the dead are buried above the ground in structures called mausoleums, which are crowded close together and painted white. Since these mausoleums make New Orleans cemeteries look like small cities, they are often called "cities of the dead."

In New Orleans, the mighty Mississippi River laps gently at the shore. With its low-lying banks, the wide, slow-moving Mississippi seems to pose no danger, yet its waters can be destructive. In the past, the river flooded and overflowed its banks from time to time. For this reason, New Orleanians have built walls called levees to hold the water back. Unfortunately, these levees block the view of the Mississippi from most places in the city.

About 150 years ago, the docks along the levee were a bustling center of activity. Riverboatmen unloaded boxes and bales of goods from the rafts they had floated downriver. These goods—cotton, sugar, furs, and more—covered the levee as far as the eye could see. Magnificent paddle-wheel steamboats hugged the shore, and close beside them were tall sailing ships that had brought goods from across the Atlantic Ocean and Gulf of Mexico.

New Orleans is still one of the world's great ports. Every day, barges loaded with goods and supplies travel up and down the Mississippi River and the Gulf Intracoastal Waterway that runs along the Gulf of Mexico from Florida to Texas. More than 5,000 ships call at the Port of New Orleans every year.

The wide Mississippi River has brought trade to New Orleans throughout its history.

Jazz musicians can often be found playing on New Orleans street corners.

The rich river trade of New Orleans has always drawn people to the city. First came the French and Spanish, ancestors of the Creoles. They were followed by the Acadians, or Cajuns, from Canada and the English-speaking Americans from upriver. Free blacks migrated from Haiti, and many more black slaves were brought from the other islands in the West Indies. Waves of immigrants also came from Ireland, Germany, and Italy. This mix of cultures has given New Orleans a rich tradition of good food, good music, and good times.

Food is one of New Orleans's biggest attractions. The city's French, Spanish, and African heritage has produced two different cooking styles:

Creole and its country cousin, Cajun. Other immigrant groups have added their special dishes over the years. Today, everything from blackened redfish and gumbo (a spicy stew) to muffulettas (huge Italian sandwiches) and beignets (sweet, powdery doughnuts) fill the city streets with their delicious smells.

New Orleans also prides itself on its music. It is the city where jazz was born. Jazz, like New Orleans cooking, mixes together a little bit of this and a little bit of that, and seasons it all with a pinch of something hot and spicy. Marching bands play jazz at parades, picnics, parties, and funerals. Day and night, its sweet, sad sounds pour from open doorways on Bourbon Street and throughout the city.

There is no better time to enjoy food and music than during a festival, and New Orleans has plenty of them. The festival New Orleanians treasure the most is Mardi Gras. For two weeks each winter, everyone in the city gets caught up in the whirl and excitement of the festivities. Laughing, screaming crowds, colorful costumes, and huge floats fill the streets. Wild merrymakers dance and shout at the parades winding through the city. Masked kings, clowns, and marchers scatter trinkets as they go.

New Orleans's reputation for fun draws millions of visitors every year. People are charmed by the mule-drawn carriages and wooden streetcars that carry them through the streets. A ride on an old Mississippi

During Mardi Gras, New Orleanians love to dress in elaborate costumes.

steamboat offers a view of the city from the river.

The city's tourist attractions are centered in the French Quarter, the oldest part of town. Spanish-style houses with lacy iron balconies line the streets of this quarter. In other parts of the city, dignified southern mansions and rambling Victorian houses remind people of other times in the city's history. Museums show old Mardi Gras costumes, wax models of pirates, voodoo charms, and rooms restored to look the way they did when people lived in them long ago. Visitors are also drawn to the city's parks, shops, and restaurants.

Even with this growing tourist business, New Orleans has experienced hard times lately. A slowdown

Many historic French Quarter streets are framed by the lacy iron balconies of Spanish-style houses.

in the city's economy caused many workers to lose their jobs. In some areas, poor people live in run-down houses that they can't afford to fix. A high crime rate makes caution part of everyday life.

Still, the city has survived difficulties in the past and is working to solve its present problems. Its citizens continue to enjoy New Orleans's special way of life, through good times and bad.

2

Creoles and Anglos

From its French and Spanish beginnings, New Orleans has been unlike any other American city. It has a flavor all its own: sharp, spicy, and slightly foreign. The variety of New Orleanians—drawn to the city from all over the world—hasn't always blended into a friendly community. But during the best of times, the city's ethnic groups have mingled together, each adding its own spice to the delicious gumbo that is New Orleans.

The French were the first Europeans to explore the mouth of the Mississippi River, in the land where the Choctaw Indians lived. In 1718, Jean Baptiste le Moyne, Sieur de Bienville, chose the site for a port city 107 miles (172 kilometers) up the river from the Gulf of Mexico. It was the first place he found that was high and dry enough to build on! In honor of

Many bayous near New Orleans still look much as they did when the French explored the area in the early 1700s.

the Duc d'Orleans, a powerful leader in the French government, he named the city New Orleans.

At first, there were many more men than women in the city. But in 1727, six Roman Catholic nuns arrived to care for the sick and start a school for girls. Soon after, the French government offered money and clothes to any poor girl who went to the new city to marry. These young women were known as *les filles à la cassette*, or casket girls, because of the *cassettes* (caskets or chests) that they carried their clothes in.

The children, grandchildren, and other descendants of the original settlers were called Creoles. Most were French-speaking Catholics. Because of the growing wealth of New Orleans's busy port, many Creoles had money and an easy life. They enjoyed fine food, festivals, and other pleasures. From them came the pleasant, colorful way of life that New Orleans is famous for.

Another group of French-speaking people came to the city from Acadia, a colony in Canada. The Acadians were forced to leave their homeland by the British, and many of them settled just outside New Orleans. Over time, the name *Acadian* was shortened to *Cajun*. Cajuns still live in the countryside around New Orleans, farming and fishing on the bayous, or small rivers or streams.

Black people have lived in New Orleans almost from its beginning. Most were slaves brought from Afri-

This landscape from the early 1800s shows how the Acadian settlers lived on the Louisiana bayous.

ca or from French colonies in the Caribbean Sea. Others were the children of slave mothers and Creole fathers—they were known as "free persons of color." Some free blacks were rich and well educated, while many others were skilled workers, especially in the building trades.

Spain took control of the city in the mid-1700s, yet life in New Orleans didn't change much. Few Spaniards moved to the city, and the Creoles continued to speak French. The biggest effect the Spanish had on New Orleans resulted from a terrible fire on March 21, 1788, which destroyed four-fifths of the city's buildings. The Spaniards replaced them with the style of building they knew best. This is why today Spanish houses crowd the streets of the French Quarter, the oldest part of town.

In 1803, the United States government bought New Orleans as part of the Louisiana Purchase. Soon the city was swarming with "Anglos," the English-speaking Americans from the north. Creoles had a low opinion of Anglos because most Anglos they had known were loud, drunken riverboatmen from places upriver, such as Kentucky. The Creoles called them all "Kaintocks."

Not all Anglos were like the riverboatmen. Most were strict Protestants who disapproved of the free-and-easy ways of the Creoles. To Creoles, Sunday was a day for fun and relaxation, while to the Protestant Anglos, Sunday was for church only. In order to make things easier for everyone, the Anglos moved uptown, and the Creoles stayed downtown. Canal Street was the dividing line, and for many years each side tried to have as little to do with the other as possible.

Pirates were also part of life in early New Orleans. Jean Lafitte and his wild crew had their headquarters in the swamps around Barataria Bay south of the city. They smuggled, looted, burned, fought, and killed. In 1813, Governor William Claiborne of Louisiana offered $500 for Lafitte's arrest. The pirate captain promptly offered $1,500 to anyone who would arrest the governor.

During the War of 1812, Jean Lafitte had his chance to be a hero. When the British threatened to invade New Orleans, Lafitte offered to provide men and supplies for the city's defense. General Andrew Jackson, the leader of the American forces, knew he couldn't be too strict about who joined his troops. Against the large, well-trained British army, he needed all the help he could get. His ragged army of pirates, free blacks, Choctaw Indians, Anglos, and Creoles fought bravely. When the Battle of New Orleans was over on January 8, 1815, more than 2,000 British

Modern-day patriots re-enact the Battle of New Orleans.

The steamboat increased the trade to New Orleans's port and brought much wealth to the city.

soldiers lay dead or wounded, but fewer than 80 Americans. The Americans had won, and the pirate Lafitte received a pardon. Unfortunately, neither side knew that the war had officially ended more than two weeks earlier.

The golden age of New Orleans began with the end of this war and lasted for the next 50 years. It was built on a three-part base—sugar, cotton, and the steamboat. Sugar and cotton were grown on great plantations in the countryside near New Orleans and shipped out of its port. Steamboats made the port one of the busiest in the country, because for the first time a boat could travel *up* the river as easily as it could travel down.

New Orleans became a center of

great activity. Steamboats and sailing ships from Europe crowded four-deep along the levees. Visitors came from all over the world, and immigrants began arriving from Germany, Ireland, and, later, Italy. Even the Choctaw Indians came to the city to sell sassafras roots and homemade baskets.

By 1820, 27,000 people lived in New Orleans. Of these, 7,000 were slaves, and almost as many were free persons of color. Slave trading meant big business; smugglers brought slaves into the city from hiding places in the swamps, and slaves were sold throughout town, even in the lobbies of elegant hotels.

New Orleans's swampy location and poor sanitation were a major problem throughout the 1800s. Al-most every summer, yellow fever—a terrible disease carried by mosquitoes from nearby swamps—and cholera spread through the city. Poor people were the main victims. During 1853, the worst year, almost one-tenth of the city's population died.

New Orleanians did their best to ignore these deadly diseases and enjoy their city's wealth instead. People who weren't sick, poor, or slaves amused themselves with dinner parties, plays, masquerades (parties where everyone wore masks), and luxurious balls. Special balls were even held for children as young as four.

The parties stopped in 1861 when Louisiana seceded, or withdrew, from the Union and the Civil

Before the Civil War, wealthy New Orleanians entertained frequently, often in beautifully furnished rooms like this one.

War began. No major battles were fought around New Orleans, but one year later the city was occupied by Union forces led by Major General Benjamin Butler. Most white New Orleanians hated Butler and his troops—even wealthy ladies insulted soldiers on the streets. Yet the city remained in Union hands until the end of the war.

Newly freed slaves flocked to the city after the Civil War. Public schools were opened to both black and white children. For the first time, black people could vote and hold office. Even though blacks and whites were still kept separate in most public places, many white New Orleanians would not accept these changes and responded with violence. In 1866, 34

blacks were killed by police when they gathered for a political meeting. During the rest of the century, a dishonest political organization known as the Ring ran the city government.

Yet out of this troubled time at least one good thing was born—jazz. No one is quite sure when jazz started, but by the early 1900s it was being played nightly throughout the city's Storyville district, an area of bars, gambling, and illegal activities. Different pieces of New Orleans's musical past are mixed into jazz: African chants and drum rhythms, slave songs, marches, ragtime, the blues, and classical music. The blacks in Storyville mixed these pieces together to create a new American musical form.

Along with jazz, the early 1900s gave birth to a wide range of improvements, including better city sewers and water supply systems. Before 1900, New Orleans had been one of the dirtiest cities in the country. Garbage and other wastes were dumped into the river across from downtown. Very poor people had to drink the unhealthy river water, but most houses had small tanks, called cisterns, to collect rainwater for drinking. The new sewers and water purifying plant meant that clean water was available for everyone at last.

The city also began improving its port and building new barges and towboats. These improvements made the Mississippi more useful, but not less dangerous. Flooding was a problem— nine times in its history, the river had burst the levees upriver and washed over New Orleans. Finally, in 1931, the U.S. government built the Bonnet Carré Spillway about 30 miles (48 kilometers) west of New Orleans. When flooding threatens, this channel can move 250 million cubic feet (7 million cubic meters) of water per second from the Mississippi to Lake Pontchartrain. As a result, flooding is no longer a threat to New Orleans.

Other dangers threatened the city, though. World War II was as close as the Gulf of Mexico. German submarines waited near the mouth of the Mississippi and in 1942 sunk 13 ships, some from New Orleans.

Almost 20 years later, violence broke out when four black girls, protected by U.S. marshals, started school in an all-white elementary school. Because blacks and whites had lived separately for almost one hundred years, integration was difficult at first. Yet blacks, who make up more than half the city's population, were soon taking part in city government. In 1977, Ernest Morial became the city's first black mayor.

The city government was soon to face serious problems. For several decades, New Orleans's fortunes had depended heavily on oil and natural gas found offshore in the Gulf of Mexico, and on the processing of minerals, chemicals, and oil. During the mid-1980s, these industries were hurt by a drop in oil prices, and many people lost their jobs. Today, giant oil rigs sit empty in the canals and bayous

An oil refinery near New Orleans.

around the city, while the people who ran them wait to return to work.

Throughout this century, New Orleans has grown, its suburbs have expanded, and bridges and office buildings have been built. Yet the city is no longer as important as it was when it was the largest southern city. Today other cities are larger, wealthier, and more powerful. Still, bigger and richer doesn't mean more interesting. New Orleans is admired not for its size, but for its character and charm.

3

Above and Below Canal Street

From the Mississippi River to Lake Pontchartrain, Canal Street divides New Orleans neatly in two. Native New Orleanians use Canal Street as a guide in locating places. They call the area to the northeast "Below Canal" and to the southwest "Above Canal."

In some ways, Canal Street pulls the city together. Like any main street, it's a center of business. Stores, restaurants, hotels, and office buildings line both of its sides. And every year at carnival time, all New Orleans comes to Canal Street to celebrate the fun and excitement of Mardi Gras.

But Canal Street divides the city more than it unites it. Streets change their names when they cross Canal. Once Bourbon Street goes above Canal, it becomes Carondelet. Royal Street becomes St. Charles Avenue. At one time, only Creoles lived below

Today Canal Street is a center of business; in the past it divided the city in two.

The spires of the St. Louis Cathedral rise over Jackson Square in the heart of the French Quarter.

Canal, and only Anglos lived above Canal. New Orleanians still call the large islands in the center of Canal Street "neutral grounds."

Because New Orleans began at the Mississippi, the oldest neighborhoods border the river. Directly below Ca-

nal is the French Quarter, or *Vieux Carré* (Old Square), as the Creoles called it. This is where the French founded the original city. On some of its streets, old Spanish-style houses stand quietly in the sun. Other streets are more lively. The jazz playing day and night on Bourbon Street often makes it sound like one long party.

At the heart of the French Quarter lies Jackson Square, where a statue of Andrew Jackson rises over the city he once defended. An iron fence encloses the park in the center of the square. Artists lean their canvases against this fence while they paint. Visitors photograph the sights, and clowns and musicians stroll among them, stopping now and then to perform.

Three famous New Orleans buildings stand at one end of Jackson Square. The Cabildo, once home of the Spanish government, and the Presbytère are now part of the Louisiana State Museum. The third building, the St. Louis Cathedral, is still in use as a Roman Catholic church.

Mimes, who silently act out stories, entertain visitors to Jackson Square.

Down both sides of Jackson Square stand two rows of attached houses containing shops and apartments. The Pontalba Apartments were built about 1850 by the Baroness Micaela Pontalba to bring business back to the fading Vieux Carré. At a time when ladies didn't do such things, the Baroness, dressed in trousers, would climb ladders to inspect the workmen's progress. Today these buildings still contain some of the most desirable apartments in the city.

Buildings throughout the French Quarter are beautiful, and many people take walking tours of the area just to look at them. Romantic old houses press close against the banquettes, as sidewalks are called in New Orleans. Lacy iron railings decorate the second-story galleries, or balconies. Narrow alleys separate the houses, and behind them, almost invisible from the street, lie cool, dim courtyards filled with tropical plants.

North and northwest of the French Quarter are two other old neighborhoods: Trémé and Faubourg Marigny. Creole cottages are common in these areas. Each small, square cottage has four rooms, no halls, and a patio in the back. Many black Creoles still live in these houses. Andrew Young, the mayor of Atlanta, was born in this part of the city. So was Louis Armstrong, the "father of jazz" and New Orleans's most famous son. And jazz, too, was born here—in the area once known as Storyville.

The bars and run-down hotels of

Storyville were torn down long ago. They have been replaced by the quiet ponds and rolling lawns of Louis Armstrong Park. Here, a statue of the great trumpet player overlooks Beauregard Square. Before the Civil War, this square was known as Congo Square. Black people would gather here on Sunday afternoons to dance and play the music of their native Africa.

Directly above Canal is the Central Business District (also called the CBD), the oldest uptown neighborhood in New Orleans. Like many of the city's neighborhoods, it was once a plantation that was sold and divided into building lots. The Anglos settled in this neighborhood, and it grew rapidly until, by the mid-1800s, it was the leading business section of the city.

The statue of Louis Armstrong, New Orleans's own "father of jazz," in Beauregard Square.

Today, the CBD bustles with the activity of the many people who work there. New skyscrapers sparkle in the sunlight: the World Trade Center with its revolving top, the Canal Place shopping center, and many luxury hotels. The Louisiana Convention Center was built on the site of the 1984 World's Fair. So was Riverwalk, a complex of shops and restaurants that offers live music and stunning views of the Mississippi River.

At the edge of the CBD stands the Louisiana Superdome, the world's largest indoor sports arena. Local football fans flock here to cheer the Saints, and fans from all over the United States come to watch the college teams playing in the Sugar Bowl Classic on New Year's Day. Inside the Superdome, football is played on an artificial surface nicknamed Mardi Grass. Outside, people often exercise by walking or jogging nearly half a mile around the arena.

From the CBD, wooden streetcars clatter up St. Charles Avenue to the Garden District. More than 150 years old, the St. Charles streetcar line is the oldest railroad running with uninterrupted service in the United States. When it was founded, its owners had to promise that its trains would never go faster than four miles (six kilometers) an hour!

In the Garden District, Southern mansions line the tree-shaded streets. Unlike the Spanish-style Creole houses in the French Quarter, these American-style houses are set back

The Superdome, home of the New Orleans Saints, lies alongside the Central Business District.

from the street and surrounded by wide lawns and beautiful gardens.

Parallel to St. Charles Avenue, but closer to the river, is Magazine Street with its many antique shops. This street separates the wealthy Garden District from the working-class Irish Channel neighborhood. Irish and German immigrants once settled here. Today it is home to poor blacks and immigrants from Cuba, Vietnam, and Central America.

Like other working-class areas in New Orleans, the Irish Channel has

These long, narrow houses, called "shotgun" houses, are found in many New Orleans neighborhoods.

many narrow houses which are only one room wide and anywhere from three to seven rooms long. Each room lines up one behind the other in these "shotgun" houses. This style earned its name because, if someone fired a shotgun through the front door, the bullet would go straight through each room and out the back door without hitting anything.

New Orleans includes many other distinct neighborhoods. The University Area, farther up St. Charles Avenue, is home to Audubon Park, with its world-class zoo, and two major schools. Tulane University is called the "Harvard of the South," and Loyola University is the largest Roman Catholic university in the United States. Creoles and Italians live in Mid-City, a neighborhood that boasts both City Park, the largest park in New Orleans, and Bayou St. John. Neighborhood people like to fish in this bayou, even though they don't catch much!

Many New Orleanians picnic at Lakefront, an area along the shores of Lake Pontchartrain. On Lakeshore Drive, colored lights shine brightly through the enormous tower of water that the Mardi Gras fountain sprays into the air. The fountain, built in 1962, is dedicated to "the enjoyment of the people of and visitors to New Orleans."

Finally, there's Algiers, a neighborhood filled with quaint Victorian houses. Although Algiers is on the other side of the Mississippi from the rest of New Orleans's neighborhoods, it's still very much a part of the city. The young professionals who live here can commute across the river on the Greater New Orleans Bridge or on the free Canal Street Ferry.

New Orleans's newer neighborhoods spread farther and farther away from the city's center, and they resemble typical American suburbs. Yet it is the older neighborhoods that have won the admiration of New Orleanians and visitors alike.

4

The Big Easy

The people of New Orleans call their city the "Big Easy" and the "City that Care Forgot" because they like to enjoy themselves. "*Laissez les bon temps rouler*," they say. "Let the good times roll." New Orleanians love old houses good food, music, and the festivals that celebrate these things. Most of all, they love Mardi Gras.

In French, *mardi* means "Tuesday" and *gras* means "fat." Mardi Gras, or Fat Tuesday, is the day before Ash Wednesday, the beginning of the Christian season of Lent. Because at one time Roman Catholics were not allowed to eat meat during Lent, they had to eat all their meat and meat fats on "Fat Tuesday." In many Catholic countries, Mardi Gras became a time of carnival (the word *carnival* comes from two Latin words that mean "to remove meat"). It was

Mardi Gras, New Orleans's midwinter festival, is a time of colorful parades.

a day of feast and festivity before the Lenten fast. In New Orleans, the carnival of Mardi Gras lasts two weeks. The remaining fifty weeks of the year are spent getting ready!

Mardi Gras merrymaking, New Orleans-style, began in 1857 when a group of young men who called themselves the Mystick Krewe of Comus organized a parade. Their parade was led by a comical, masked king—Comus, the Roman god of mirth. Since then, all of the city's carnivals have been run by organizations called krewes and have featured parades, masks, and kings.

Every year during Mardi Gras, masked figures such as Comus, Rex, Momus, Proteus, Bacchus, Zulu, and Iris lead parades of gaily colored floats and brilliantly costumed riders along Canal Street. Excited people crowd the street, screaming, "Throw me something, mister!" Everyone, especially the children, tries to catch "throws"—small gifts of doubloons (metal coins), beads, or plastic caps showing a krewe's emblem—that people on the floats toss to the crowds.

King cakes are another Mardi Gras custom. Each cake has a tiny doll or bean hidden inside. All New Orleans bakeries sell them during the two months before Mardi Gras, and people eat them at king cake parties. Whoever gets the doll or bean is supposed to host the next party.

No one is sure when or how the custom of Mardi Gras "Indians" began, but for many years "tribes" of black people—mostly young men, but some women and children, too—have appeared on New Orleans's streets during Mardi Gras dressed in fancy American Indian costumes. From sunrise on, these merrymakers roam the streets looking for each other. Whenever two groups meet, they greet each other with dances and songs.

Although parades brighten almost every day, the Mardi Gras festivities don't hit their peak until the evening of Lundi Gras, "Fat Monday." That's when Mardi Gras officially begins as the king, Rex, and his court arrive by Mississippi riverboat and set off a fireworks display.

The next day, Fat Tuesday, is an official holiday. Schools and offices

These young New Orleanians are dressed to enjoy the custom of Mardi Gras "Indians."

are closed, and everyone rushes to the street to watch parades. Many in the crowd also wear masks and costumes, in the hopes of winning a contest. Neighborhood marching clubs and brass bands add to the noise and excitement. Private balls are held in the evening. Finally, at the stroke of midnight, all celebrations stop—Mardi Gras ends as Lent begins.

The New Orleans Jazz and Heritage Festival, the city's second largest festival, takes place about one month later. For two weekends in the spring, about three hundred musical groups play all types of music at the New Orleans Fairgrounds racetrack—gospel, soul, rhythm and blues, folk, rock and roll, bluegrass, zydeco (a type of Cajun accordian music), Lat-

in, blues, ragtime, country and western, and, of course, jazz.

One way to learn more about New Orleans jazz is to see the jazz history exhibit housed in the Old U.S. Mint Building. An even better way is to hear it played by some of the original musicians at Preservation Hall in the French Quarter. The best way is to "second line." Second-lining is a New Orleans tradition. New Orleanians don't just watch a marching jazz band. Instead, adults and children alike form a "second line" behind and around the musicians and follow along, dancing, spinning, strutting, and sashaying as they go. Whenever they hear band music, many New Orleanians and visitors may be tempted to drop what they're doing to run to

Old-style New Orleans jazz is played nightly at Preservation Hall.

the street and second line.

Shortly after Easter, a parade and the crowning of a queen kick off New Orleans's third major festival. For the five days of Spring Fiesta, visitors can tour some of the houses from New Orleans's past that are nor-mally closed to the public. Home-owners in the French Quarter and Garden District open their doors in welcome. Organizations arrange tours to Creole houses and many of the old plantations that line the River Road just west of New Orleans. Some

Like many plantations near New Orleans, Nottoway gives visitors a glimpse of life before the Civil War.

plantations even allow visitors to stay overnight—a pleasant way to go back in time and sample daily life on a plantation as it was before the Civil War.

Some of the city's festivals were started by the different ethnic groups that lived there, although today New Orleanians of all kinds enjoy them. On St. Patrick's Day, the Irish celebrate, and on Bastille Day, the French. During the Festa d'Italia and on St. Joseph's Day, the Italians pile their altars high with food. Other celebrations put a New Orleans spin on traditional holidays. On Halloween, children tour a haunted house in City Park or take part in a special program at the Audubon Zoo ("Boo-at-the-Zoo"). A "Creole Christmas" includes candlelight carols in Jackson Square. Farther up the Mississippi, bonfires along the levee light the way for Papa Noel, the French version of Santa Claus. Fireworks explode over the river on New Year's Eve.

Almost every celebration offers a chance to sample New Orleans's world-famous Creole and Cajun cooking. Some festivals, though, are held mainly to give people a chance to eat. Both La Fête and the Food Festival allow dozens of chefs to cook and serve a wide variety of dishes. Creole cooking is usually done with lots of garlic, hot pepper, and sauces, particularly sauces made from a roux—fat and flour heated and stirred until it darkens and thickens. Typical Creole dishes are blackened redfish, gumbo, and jambalaya (a rice dish with different kinds of meat and shellfish).

Cajun cooking is similar to Creole, but it is heartier and spicier with fewer sauces. Both styles of cooking feature seafood—shrimp, oysters, crabs, redfish, and crawfish (crayfish), which look like small lobsters. According to New Orleanians, the best way to eat crawfish is to "squeeze the tips and suck the heads."

Two New Orleans specialties—po'boys and muffulettas—resemble what are known in other cities as heros, submarines, or grinders. A po'boy is a loaf of French bread filled with meat or seafood and lettuce, tomatoes, pickles, and mayonnaise. Fried oysters are a favorite filling, and so is roast beef with lots of gravy—the sloppier, the better. A muffuletta is a thick round loaf of Italian bread that is split in half and layered with ham, spicy cold cuts, two kinds of cheese, and olive salad.

Two sweet New Orleans foods are for sale at the French Market, a 200-year-old trading place that now houses restaurants, cafes, and shops. Beignets—square, holeless doughnuts—are a favorite New Orleans snack with coffee or hot chocolate. Another favorite is pralines, a candy made with pecans and brown sugar.

There is plenty to see and do in the French Quarter besides eat. People often like to tour the many sights on foot. In one museum, the Musée Conti, life-size wax figures present scenes from New Orleans's history, including the signing of the Louisiana Purchase and the Battle of New Orleans. One exhibit shows a cruel slave-owner, Madame Lalaurie, who beat and starved her slaves until she was forced to leave town. Her house, also located in the French Quarter, is said to be haunted by their ghosts.

The Voodoo Museum shows another interesting side of New Orleans's history. Many blacks in the city's early years practiced voodoo, a blend of African religions and Catholicism. The most famous voodoo priestess was Marie Laveau. Many

Beignets, a favorite New Orleans treat, are sold at a 125-year-old cafe in the French Market.

people came to her for advice and to buy gris-gris charms for good and evil. A favorite good-luck gris-gris was a dime with a hole in it, worn around the ankle.

Outside the French Quarter, the city's two great parks are wonderful places to walk. Audubon Park, where the zoo is located, was named for John James Audubon, the artist and naturalist. The park's 400 acres (160 hectares) were originally two plantations. One of them belonged to Etienne de Boré, an early New Orleanian

White alligators can be seen only in the Audubon Zoo.

who first discovered how to form sugar into crystals on a large scale.

Today, the Audubon Zoo is one of the park's main attractions. A miniature train travels through the zoo, past animals in natural settings. The Louisiana Swamp Exhibit offers a glimpse of the plant and animal life of southern Louisiana. It's the only zoo in the world with white alligators.

Monkey Hill was built in Audubon Park during the 1930s, but it wasn't always part of the zoo. Once, children used to play on its 50-foot

(15-meter) high slopes because it was the only hill in all of New Orleans. But the zoo expanded during the 1970s, and Monkey Hill is now part of its African Savannah exhibit.

City Park, one of the largest parks in a U.S. city, also began as a sugar plantation. The New Orleans Museum of Art is located here. So are the Dueling Oaks, an area that earned its name during the 1700s when dueling was common. Men armed with swords, pistols, and other deadly weapons came to this large group of oak trees and attempted to settle their disagreements by killing each other. Also located in City Park is a beautiful old carousel. Built in 1904, it has recently been repainted and restored. New

Orleans children can ride its prancing horses as their parents and grandparents did before them.

With parks to play in, fascinating old buildings and neighborhoods to explore, good food to eat, wonderful music to listen to, and festivals all year long, it's not hard to see how New Orleans acquired its many nicknames. Life may not always be easy in the Big Easy. Difficult times in New Orleans's past and present show that it's not really the City that Care Forgot. Still, New Orleanians like to concentrate on the good things about their city, not the bad.

Who can blame them? ''Let the good times roll!''

Places to Visit in New Orleans

Louisiana State Museum Complex

The following buildings are part of the complex:

The Arsenal
615 St. Peter Street
Firefighting equipment and military history

The Cabildo
701 Chartres Street
Early New Orleans history

Jackson House
619 St. Peter Street
Louisiana folk art

The Lower Pontalba
523 St. Ann Street
(504) 568-6968
Includes the restored 1850 House

Madame John's Legacy
632 Dumaine Street
(504) 581-4321
Restored 1788 cottage and architecture exhibit

Old U.S. Mint Building
400 Esplanade Avenue
Jazz, mint, and Mardi Gras museums

The Presbytère
751 Chartres Street
Varied exhibits, including antique toys

For information on special education programs, call or write:

Louisiana State Museum Complex
751 Chartres Street
New Orleans, LA 70116
(504) 568-6968

Other Museums

Louisiana Children's Museum
428 Julia Street
(504) 523-1357

Musée Conti Wax Museum
917 Conti Street
(504) 525-2605
Historical wax figures and Haunted Dungeon

New Orleans Museum of Art
Lelong Avenue, City Park
(504) 488-2631

Pharmacy Museum
514 Chartres Street
(504) 524-9077
Drugstore, medical, and voodoo displays

Voodoo Museum
724 Dumaine Street
(504) 523-7685
Combined museum and store (voodoo supplies)

Plantations near New Orleans

Destrehan
9999 River Road, Destrehan, LA
(504) 764-9315

San Francisco
LA Highway 44 near Reserve, LA
(504) 535-2341

Houmas House
River Road, Burnside, LA
(504) 522-2262

Nottoway
LA 1, 2 miles north of White Castle, LA
(504) 545-2730

Parks

Audubon Park and Zoological Garden
6500 Magazine Street
(504) 861-2537

Chalmette National Historical Park
St. Bernard Highway, Chalmette, LA
(504) 589-4428
Site of the Battle of New Orleans

City Park
Intersection of North Carrollton, Wisner,
and Esplanade avenues
(504) 482-4888

Louisiana Nature Center
11000 Lake Forest Boulevard
(504) 246-9381

Performing Arts

Children's Corner of Little Theatre
616 St. Peter Street
(504) 522-1954

New Orleans Philharmonic Symphony
Orchestra
Orpheum Theatre
129 University Place
(504) 524-0404
Special performances for children

Pontalba Historical Puppetorium
514 St. Peter Street
(504) 522-0344
Puppets re-enact the story of pirate Jean Lafitte

Steamboat Rides

Bayou Jean Lafitte, Cotton Blossom, Steamboat Natchez, Riverboat President
New Orleans Steamboat Company
(504) 586-8777

Creole Queen
New Orleans Paddlewheels, Inc.
(504) 529-4567

Voyageur
Louisiana Cruises, Inc.
(504) 523-5555

Special Sites

Louisiana Superdome
1500 Poydras Street
(504) 587-3810
Daily tours

St. Louis Cemetery No. 1
Basin and St. Louis streets

St. Louis Cemetery No. 2
North Claiborne Avenue

Additional information can be obtained from these agencies:

Greater New Orleans Tourist and
Convention Commission
1520 Sugar Bowl Drive
New Orleans, LA 70112
(504) 566-5011

Chamber of Commerce
New Orleans & The River Region
P.O. Box 30240
New Orleans, LA 70190
(504) 527-6900

New Orleans: A Historical Time Line

1699   French explorers Pierre and Jean le Moyne reach what is now called the Mississippi River

1718   Jean Baptiste le Moyne, Sieur de Bienville, founds New Orleans

1722   New Orleans becomes the capital of French Louisiana

1727   Roman Catholic nuns arrive in the city to start a girl's school

1762   France gives New Orleans to Spain

1788   Fire destroys almost four-fifths of the city

1795   Etienne de Boré discovers how to make sugar into crystals on a large scale; sugar production becomes an important industry

1800   Spain gives Louisiana, including New Orleans, back to France

1803   France sells New Orleans to the United States as part of the Louisiana Purchase

1812   Louisiana becomes a state; the first steamboat arrives in New Orleans from upriver; the War of 1812 begins

1815   General Andrew Jackson defeats the British at the Battle of New Orleans

1831   New Orleans's first railroad line opens

1841   New Orleans's first city-and-state supported free schools are established

1850-51 The Pontalba Apartments are built

1853   Yellow fever epidemic takes almost 8,000 lives

1857   First Mardi Gras organization, the Mystick Krewe of Comus, is formed

1861   Louisiana secedes from the Union; Civil War begins

1862   Union troops occupy New Orleans

1866	Police fire upon free blacks outside Mechanic's Institute, killing 34
1868	Blacks in New Orleans vote and hold office for the first time
1877	Union troops withdraw from the city
1884	World Industrial and Cotton Centennial Exposition opens in what is now Audubon Park
1908	New Orleans's first sewer system goes into operation
1909	Water purifying plant is built to supply the city with clean water
1917	Storyville is closed; jazz moves upriver and becomes popular in other cities
1921	Inner Harbor Navigation Canal is dug to provide a water route from the Mississippi River to Lake Pontchartrain
1931	U.S. government constructs Bonnet Carré Spillway to control flooding
1942	During World War II, 13 ships are sunk by the Germans in the Gulf of Mexico near New Orleans
1960	New Orleans public schools are integrated
1975	Louisiana Superdome is completed
1977	Ernest Morial becomes New Orleans's first black mayor
1984	The World's Fair is held in New Orleans
1986	New Orleans's unemployment rate rises to above 11 percent
1988	Republican National Convention is held in New Orleans to choose a presidential candidate

A New Orleans Glossary

New Orleanians frequently have their own way of saying things. Here are some expressions that are used in the Crescent City.

banquette (ban·KEHT)—a sidewalk

bayou (BY·yoo)—a small river or stream, usually marshy

beignet (bihn·YAY)—a square, powdered doughnut

Cajun (KAY·juhn)—a person descended from the French-Canadians who came to Louisiana in the late eighteenth century

crawfish (or crayfish)—a tasty shellfish that looks like a small lobster

Creole (KREE·ohl)—a person descended from early French and Spanish settlers

gallerie—an outdoor balcony or porch

gris-gris (gree·gree)—a voodoo charm that brings either good or bad luck

krewe (kroo)—a social club that sponsors Mardi Gras activities

lagniappe (lan·YAP)—something extra thrown in for good measure

levee (LEHV·ee)—a dike, or wall, built alongside a river to prevent flooding

muffuletta—an Italian-style oval sandwich made with cold cuts, cheese, and olive salad on a roll

neutral ground—median or divider in the center of a street, especially Canal Street

po' boy (or poor boy)—a sandwich made with fillings such as roast beef or oysters on French bread

shotgun house—a long, narrow house with rooms in a straight line, one behind the other

"Where y'at?"—a greeting that means "Hello! How are you?"

Index